FISH
AND
MOOSE
NEWS

FISH AND MOOSE NEWS

Cartoons by Bill Woodman

DODD, MEAD & COMPANY · NEW YORK

Of the 111 drawings in this book, twenty-three appeared originally in *The New Yorker*
and were copyrighted © in 1975, 1976, 1977, 1978, and 1979 by The New Yorker
Magazine, Inc.
Cartoons appearing on pages 51 and 59 are copyrighted © in 1977 by *Playboy* and are
used with their permission.
The artist also wishes to thank *Audubon Magazine* for permission to use those drawings of his for which they hold the copyright.

This book's first cartoon appears on page 7.

Library of Congress Cataloging in Publication Data

Woodman, Bill.
  Fish and moose news.

  1. American wit and humor, Pictorial. I. Title.
NC1429.W64A4   1980   741.5'973   79-27794
ISBN 0-396-07825-7

To Fred and Ada

"All right, fellas, are you ready for this year's rules?"

"Oh, what a beautiful mornin'! Oh, what a beautiful day! . . ."

"Poor Ralph. His sons are getting old and yet they're still not ready
to face the world."

"Something tells me we won't forget this season for awhile."

OODMAN

WOODMAN

WOODMAN

WOODMAN

WOODMAN

WOODMAN

BANK

WOODMAN

"What will it be?"

"Just pick it up, honey, and say hello."

"Moose alert."

WOODMAN

"The boys seem to be getting along just fine."
"I see the girls are getting along all right."

"What's your dog's name?"

WOODMAN

"Come on. We'll go ashore, have a little fun and be back by sunset.
It'll be good for you."

"All business and no play. Wouldn't you agree, Professor?"

"Of course, right now it's only up and down, but we're working on
the somersault."

WOODMAN

WOODMAN

"Did you ever have one of those mornings when you just couldn't hack it? The 'Times,' I mean."

WOODMAN

WOODMAN

"Two scrambled."

"How's this for fun?"

"Looks like Clement got the talent in this family."

"Well, just supposing you did get her up there. What makes you
think people would come to see her?"

"Young man, you're wasting your time up there. She ran off with Mr. Peavey a week ago last Tuesday."

WOODMAN

"Looks like Jed's got himself quite a handful this morning."

"You don't have to tell me that I don't get any calls here. I know I never get any calls here. I'm just saying that should I get any calls here, just say that I'm not here."

"Not what you'd call your most agreeable situation, wouldn't you agree?"

"This next piece is dedicated to you carrots over there."

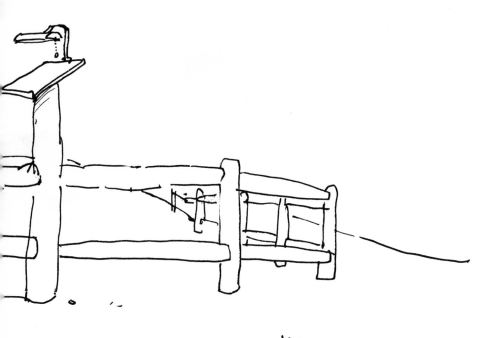

"I heard that same sea story over 300 years ago."

"Keep an eye out for rapids."

"Potato!"

"It looks like we're coming into potato country."

"I can see you, <u>that's</u> who!"

WOODMAN

"Here come some more. Let's all look edible."

"Just remember, dear, next summer you'll be able to look back at all this and laugh."

"These look like the famous L.L. Bean's Maine hunting shoes."

"Eggs, Benedict?"

WOODMAN

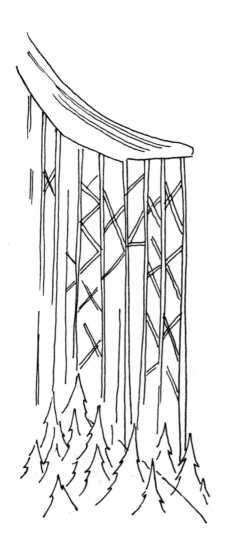

"Gentlemen, the king would like a laugh."

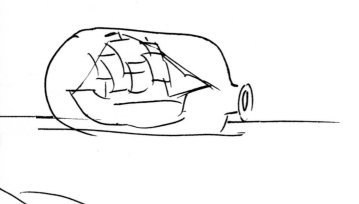

WOODMAN

WOODMAN

"Now what?"

"You could have franks and beans,
cold cuts, spaghetti and meat balls,
a mess of beet greens, crabmeat salad,
native corn . . .

"...or cheeseburgers, hot dogs, string beans, cabbage salad, with blueberry pie."

"Relax, fella. We'll get to you."

"The dinner was great, but they're certainly no barrel of laughs."

"What do you expect? I told you if you're going to have a yard sale
you've got to advertise!"

"Your mom's a very special person."

SEA GULL
ROCK

"Hey, Elmer. Put that coffee to ya!"

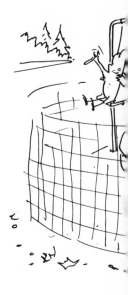

"It just won't be the same around here after the holidays."

"I just want you to know that of all the people I've met tonight, I think you're the most interesting."

"Hi, hon. Did you bring home the bacon?"

"This one here is my National League, and that one over there is
my American League."

WOODMAN

"Just up from the city?"

"This is the kind of weather I like, lots of action."

"Bravo, bravo!"

"Well, now, if no one objects, I think I'll be off to bed."